3

About this book

Light travels faster than anything in the universe. It has energy. It enables us to see objects, colours and shadows. It can play some curious tricks on our eyes. You can see how fantastic light is by doing the experiments in this book. If you are not familiar with something you need for an experiment, look on p.6 for an explanation. Always read 'Laboratory procedure' on p.7 before you start an experiment.

Contents

Cover illustration Tom Stimpson

Series editor Wendy Boase
Designer Judith Escreet

Copyright © 1982 by Walker Books Ltd

First published in Great Britain in 1982 by
Methuen Children's Books Ltd, in association
with Walker Books.

Library of Congress Catalog Card
Number 82-80989

ISBN 0-688-00975-1 (pap.)
ISBN 0-688-00969-7 (lib. bdg.)

Light Fantastic

Written by
Philip Watson

Step-by-step illustrations by
Clive Scruton

Feature illustrations by
Ronald Fenton

cop 1 LOTHROP, LEE & SHEPARD BOOKS
New York

Supplies and skills

Basic materials

You don't need a lot of special equipment to experiment at home. Clear a special shelf or cupboard and start collecting some basic, inexpensive materials for your home laboratory.

Sheets of white and coloured card.

White writing paper.

Clear and coloured cellophane.

Sheets of newspaper, brown paper or old wrapping paper.

Penknife, ruler and scissors.

Soft (B or 2B) and hard (3H) pencils.

Protractor and pair of compasses.

Other materials

If you are not familiar with a particular material or piece of equipment you need for an experiment, look for it in the following list.

Batteries and holders for them are sold at radio or electrical shops. A battery's electrical energy is measured in volts.

Card is sold at art and craft shops. You can bend **stiff card**, but not **stiff, heavy card**.

Cotton wool, surgical is the kind that comes in a roll or long piece. Buy it at a chemist's shop.

Double-sided sticky tape is sold at art or craft shops. It is sticky on both sides. One side is covered by paper, which you peel off.

Dowelling is like a round wooden stick. Buy it at a hardware shop.

Flex, 2-core plastic-covered is the kind that has two strands of wire, each inside a plastic covering. Buy it at electrical or radio shops.

Food dyes colour food. Buy them at a supermarket or grocery shop.

Glass can be bought cut to size at a hardware shop or a shop that sells glass and mirror.

Gloves, surgical are tight-fitting, and made of plastic or rubber. Buy these at a chemist's shop.

Insulating tape is sold at electrical or hardware shops. It is thick and strong.

Iodine is a poisonous disinfectant. Buy it at a chemist's shop.

A light-emitting diode is like a tiny light bulb. It lights up only when electricity passes in one direction. Buy it at an electrical or radio shop.

A magnifying glass can be bought at some art and craft shops or in the science section of a large toy shop.

Masking tape won't leave a mark if peeled off gently. Buy it at an art or craft shop.

Methylated spirit is used to remove varnish. Buy it at a hardware shop.

Mirrors can be bought at a chemist's shop, or cut to size at a hardware shop or a shop that sells glass and mirror.

A modelling knife has a very sharp blade. Buy it at an art or craft shop.

Paper and paper shapes are sold at stationery shops and at art or craft shops. You can use grease-proof paper instead of **tracing paper**.

Photographic developer and fixer are sold at shops that specialise in photographic equipment.

Photographic paper may be shiny or matt finish. Never open a packet of this paper under any light other than a red safelight (see pp.38-39).

Pliers are sold at electrical or hardware shops.

Polythene is sold at hardware shops.

A resistor can be bought at an electrical or radio shop. It resists the flow of electricity in a circuit. This resistance to electricity is measured in ohms.

Sequins and beads can be bought at a haberdasher's and at some craft shops.

Strip connector is used to join electrical wiring. Buy it at an electrical or radio shop.

Switches can be bought at an electrical or hardware shop.

A washer, used in plumbing, is a small piece of metal with a central hole. Buy it at a hardware shop.

Laboratory procedure

1. The exclamation symbol means that a tool (such as a modelling knife), a material (such as iodine) or a process (such as lighting a candle) can be dangerous. If you see this symbol on any part of an experiment, always ask an adult to read through the experiment with you before you start.

2. Put on old clothes, an overall or an apron before starting.

3. Read through an experiment, then collect the materials listed.

4. Clear a work area and cover it with newspaper or other paper. Put an old wooden chopping board or cork tile on the work area if you have to cut anything.

5. Take care not to get anything in or near your eyes. If this happens, immediately rinse your eyes in clean water, and tell an adult.

6. Never eat or drink anything unless told you may do so in an experiment.

7. Clean up any mess you make.

8. Wash your hands after using a chemical, and when you have finished an experiment.

Drawing a circle

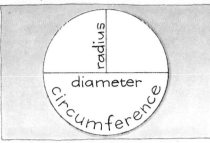

The radius is the distance between the centre of the circle and the circumference.
The diameter is double the radius.

1. Set the points of a pencil and a pair of compasses to the radius you require.

2. Put the point of the compasses firmly on a sheet of paper. It will mark the centre of the circle.

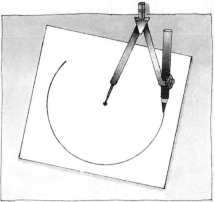

3. Swing the pencil round so that it draws a complete circle.

Drawing angles

Here's how to draw a 45° angle using a set square. Put the base of the set square on a straight line, with one 45° angle at the end of the line. Draw a line down the side of the set square to the base line.

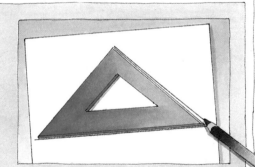

To draw 60° angles in a circle, put the centre of a protractor on the centre of the circle.

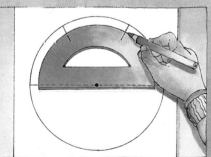

1. Find the figures 60° on the protractor and mark these two points.

2. Draw a straight line from each point, through the centre, and right across the circle.

Power of light

Light, which we get from the sun, has tremendous power. It warms the earth's entire atmosphere and provides the energy plants need to make their own food, and so provide our food. It enables us to see the plants, as well as everything else round us. The experiments in this chapter show some of light's most powerful properties at work.

Energy from light

Food-making in green plants is known as photosynthesis. The energy needed to set this process in motion comes from sunlight. See what happens to a plant deprived of light.

Materials
- geranium plant
- 2 small strips black card
- 4 paper clips
- small saucepan of boiling water
- spoon or tongs
- 50ml methylated spirit in a glass
- iodine, eye-dropper and plate

1. Clip one strip of card to each side of a large geranium leaf.

2. Put the plant on a sunny window sill for two or three days.

3. Pick the leaf and unclip the card.

4. Boil the leaf in the water for two minutes, then lift it out with the spoon. This kills the leaf.
Let the water cool to finger-hot temperature.

5. Put the leaf into the methylated spirit and stand the glass in the saucepan of hot water. This will remove the leaf's green colour.

6. When the leaf is white, put it into the hot water for 30 seconds.

7. Put the leaf on the plate and drop a few drops of iodine on to it.

Iodine turns black or very dark blue if starch is present. Starch is a source of food which plants can make only if they get light. Starch is an important part of *our* food, too. Test rice, bread, potatoes or flour with iodine. Don't eat any food that you test. Iodine is poisonous.

Power of attraction

A plant is so irresistibly attracted to light that it will twist and turn to find it. Watch this curious plant behaviour in your home laboratory.

Materials
- 10 pea or bean seeds
- saucer-sized circle of surgical cotton wool
- 2 saucers
- small jug of water
- 2 small yogurt pots filled with damp garden soil
- cardboard box with lid, painted black on the inside and about 3 times larger than 1 yogurt pot
- ruler, pencil and penknife

1. Put the cotton wool on a saucer.

2. Add enough water to soak the cotton wool but not to flood the saucer.

3. Put the seeds 1cm apart on the cotton wool.

4. Cover them with the other saucer to keep out the light, and put them in a warm place for three or four days. Keep the cotton wool moist.

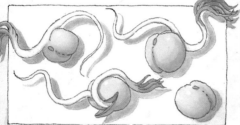

5. Look at the seeds. They should have germinated, or grown shoots. (Some may not germinate.) Germinated seeds will have a shoot with tiny leaves and a white root.

6. Use your finger to make three holes in the soil in each pot.

7. Put half the plants, root side down, into the holes in one pot, and half into the holes in the other pot.

8. Scoop soil round the plants.

9. Use the tip of the penknife to poke a small hole about half-way up one side of the box.

10. Put both pots on a well-lit window sill.

11. Cover one pot with the box.

In four of five days, you should see the uncovered plants growing upright.

12. Lift the box from the other pot.

Your plants will have bent their stems in an effort to reach the light coming through the hole in the box. This movement towards the light is called phototropism. (If the covered plants have not grown, put the box back over the pot and leave it for a few more days.)

Climbing for light

See how a plant searches for the light, even when it is upside down.

Materials
- carrot with leafy shoots
- table knife and penknife
- strong toothpick and fine string
- water

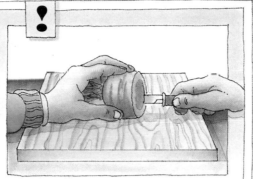

1. Use the table knife to slice through the carrot about 5cm from the leafy end.

2. Using the penknife, carefully scoop out the centre of the carrot to make a bowl with a narrow rim.

3. Push the toothpick right through the bowl of the carrot.

4. Tie equal lengths of string to each end of the toothpick.

5. Knot together the loose ends of the string, and suspend the carrot from a curtain rail or window catch in a well-lit room.

6. Fill the carrot bowl with water, and keep it topped up over the next few days.

The carrot leaves will begin to grow upward, searching for the light they need to make their own food.

Plant design

Mint is a herb used to flavour food. Next time you see some mint, look at its leaves. They are designed to catch as much light as possible. This arrangement is very important, as photosynthesis, or the process by which plants make their own food, depends on light.

Hot light

On a very warm day you can feel the strength of sunlight. If that light is concentrated through glass, it is even more powerful. Try this experiment outdoors on a sunny day.

Materials
- waste paper or dry grass
- metal tray or plate
- magnifying glass
- jug of water

1. Put the tray on a paved area, such as a path, well away from anything that could catch fire.

2. Crumple the paper and put it on the metal tray.

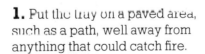

3. Hold the magnifying glass over the tray until you see a tiny, bright spot of light on the paper.

The paper will get hot, smoulder, and then glow. It will catch alight if you blow gently on it.

4. Put out the fire by pouring the jug of water on to the paper.

Mirror images

You can't see round corners because light travels only in straight lines. But light can bounce off surfaces, rather like a ball bounces off a wall. This is called reflection. Mirrors reflect light. So does white paper. You see the words on this page, for instance, because light from a lamp or the sun is reflected off the page into your eyes.

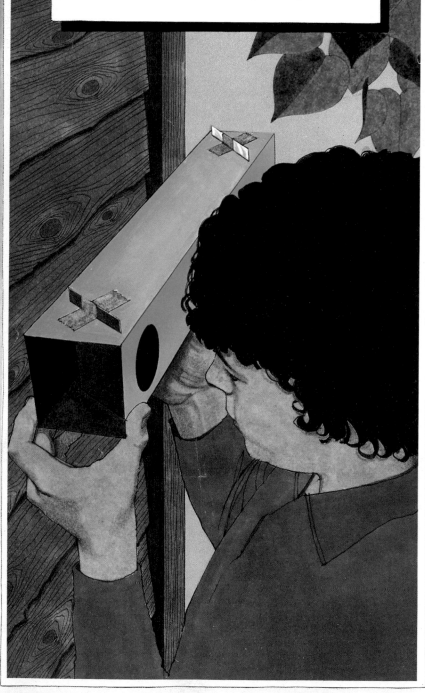

Periscope

If you make this periscope very carefully, it will enable you to see round corners and over the top of things much higher than you are.

Materials
- stiff card 28cm × 50cm, painted black on one side
- coloured pencils and ruler
- pair of compasses and scissors
- 45° set square
- masking tape
- modelling knife
- 2 mirrors, each about 7cm × 9cm

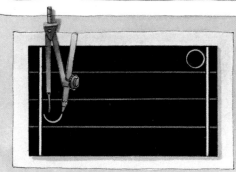

6. Draw two circles, each with a radius of 2.5cm (see p.7), as shown: touching the base lines and roughly in the centre of each panel.

7. Cut out each circle with scissors.

13. Slide a mirror through one slit so that you can see the shiny side through the opposite hole.

1. Lay the card black side up.

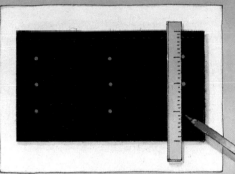

2. With the ruler parallel to the short sides, measure from the top and mark three points 7cm apart. Do this three times across the card.

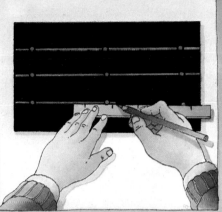

3. With the ruler parallel to the long sides, join up the marks. This divides the card into four panels.

4. Mark three points 2cm in from each short side of the card.

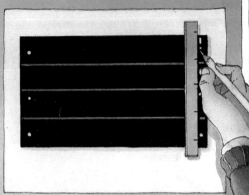

5. Join up each row of points.

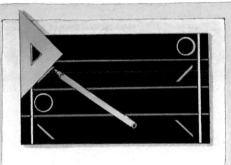

8. Use the set square (see p.7) and pencil to draw four lines, each at a 45° angle to the base line, as shown. The ends of the lines must stop 1cm from each panel line.

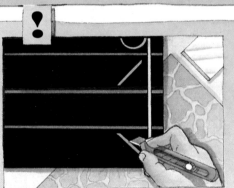

9. Slit the lines so that the short side of a mirror will fit into the slit.

10. Guided by the ruler, pull the tip of the scissors along each panel line to score it.

11. Colour or decorate the other side of the card, if you like.

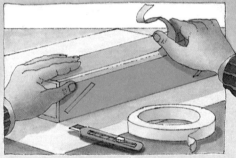

12. Fold the panels, black sides in, and tape the edges together.

14. Keep sliding the mirror until it goes through the opposite slit and is fixed in the box.

15. Fix the second mirror into the other pair of slits in the same way.

16. Tape the edges of the mirrors to the outside of the box.

17. Look through one of the holes, then point the periscope at an object above your head or round a corner.

You can see the object because light travels from it to the mirror in the top of the periscope. The light is then reflected on to the bottom mirror, and from there into your eyes.

Moonlight

Look at the moon on a clear night. It seems to shine by its own light, just as the sun does. But the moon doesn't make any light. It acts as an enormous mirror, reflecting light which travels to it from the sun.

Ambulance

Mirrors reverse everything. To read the word above, hold a mirror at the right-hand side of the word. 'Ambulance' is written back-to-front on ambulances so that other drivers can read the word when they see the vehicle in their rear-view mirrors.

Mirror writing

Mirrors can help you write secret messages in code. The famous painter Leonardo da Vinci wrote all his notes in a mirror code.

Materials
- 2 sheets writing paper
- small mirror
- pencil or pen

1. Print your message on one of the sheets of paper.

2. Hold the mirror on the paper, above the message, as shown.

True or false?

Your reflection in a mirror isn't a reliable guide to the face your friends see. Do this experiment to find out how a mirror lies, and how you can make it tell the truth.

Materials
- 2 mirrors, each about 7cm × 9cm
- masking tape and scissors

1. Hold one of the mirrors in your left hand and look at yourself.

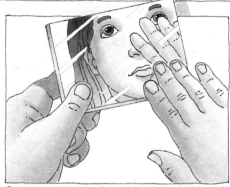

2. Lift your right hand to your face.

Your reflected image will lift its left hand!

3. Now close your left eye.

Your reflection will close its right eye!

The mirror is showing you back-to-front, or reversed, images. These images are not the ones others see when they look at you.

4. Put the shiny sides of the mirrors together.

Mirror maze

A reflection in a mirror can be very confusing. Play this game to test your skill in the mixed-up world of mirrors. Then ask some of your friends to play it!

Materials
- fairly large mirror
- sheet of writing paper
- red and green pencils or 2 different-coloured pencils
- large book

1. Use the red pencil to draw a continuous wavy line (or pattern) on the paper.

2. Prop the mirror upright on a table, or ask a friend to hold it.

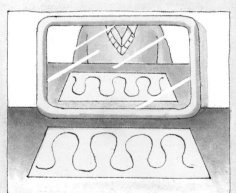

3. Lay the paper on the table so that you can see the reflection of the wavy line in the mirror.

Nobody can read the words you have written because the letters are upside down and back-to-front. This always happens if you hold a mirror above words, as shown.

3. Copy the reflected words on to the other sheet of paper.

4. Show a friend how to hold a mirror above the paper, so the message can be decoded.

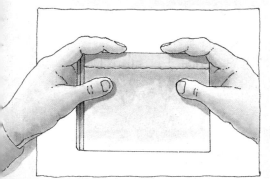

5. Tape the mirrors together along one of the longer sides.

6. Stand the mirrors upright.

7. Slowly move the mirrors together or apart until you can see one half of your face in each mirror.

8. Now lift your right hand or try closing your left eye.

This is how your friends see you!

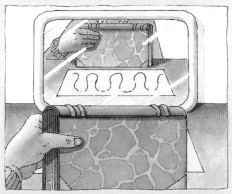

5. Look in the mirror and try to trace over your wavy line with the green pencil, using only the reflection to guide you.

Because you see a reversed image when you look in the mirror, this experiment isn't as easy as it looks!

4. Hold the book upright in front of you so that you can't see the paper itself, only its reflection.

Mirror multiplication

One object can be multiplied into many images when it is reflected in angled mirrors. You may be surprised by the effect!

Materials
- 2 mirrors, each about 7cm × 9cm
- masking tape and scissors
- pencil

1. Put the shiny sides of the mirrors together.

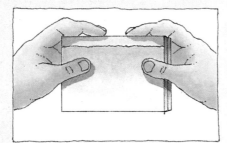

2. Tape the mirrors together along one of the longer sides.

3. Stand the mirrors upright.

4. Put the pencil down between the two mirrors. Centre the pencil so that its tip touches the point where the mirrors have been joined.
Look into the mirrors from behind the pencil.

You will see four more pencils reflected in the mirrors.

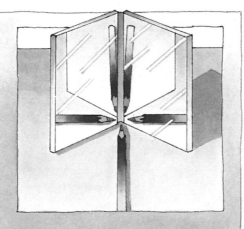

5. Slowly move the mirrors closer together, and count how many more images you can see.

When mirrors are put at certain angles to each other, a reflected image is formed in each mirror. These images reflect again on the mirrors, to form two more images. The closer the mirrors, the more images you will see.

6. Try this experiment with a flower, a straw or a pair of scissors.

Kaleidoscope

In this toy, the special arrangement of mirrors creates an endless variety of patterns.

Materials
- 2 mirrors, each 7cm × 30cm
- stiff, heavy card 7cm × 30cm, painted black on one side
- insulating tape
- ruler, pencil and scissors
- white paper 8cm square
- clear sticky tape
- colourless cellophane 16cm square
- tiny coloured paper shapes or tiny sequins and beads

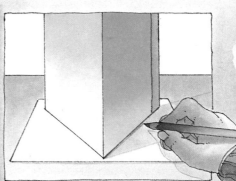

7. Stand the tube on the white paper and trace round the base.

8. Cut out the paper triangle.

13. Using clear sticky tape, join two sides of the cellophane triangles to make an envelope.

1. Using the insulating tape, fix the mirrors together as shown in step 2 of 'Mirror multiplication'.

2. Open the mirrors out flat so that the shiny sides face up.

3. Lay the card, black side down, on one mirror so that it completely covers that mirror.

4. Use insulating tape to stick the bottom edge of the card to the bottom edge of the mirror.

5. Fold the panels, shiny and black sides in, into a triangular tube.

6. Stick insulating tape across the two edges to hold them, then down the length of the tube.

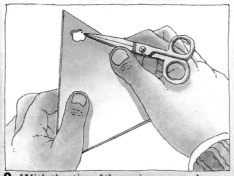

9. With the tip of the scissors, make a 1cm-diameter (see p.7) hole in one corner of the paper.

10. Put the paper over one end of the tube, with the hole between the mirrors. Fix the paper into place with clear sticky tape.

11. Hold the papered end of the kaleidoscope to your eye and look through the hole at some objects.

You will see a circular pattern of six identical images. You can achieve the same effect with coloured shapes, if you do steps 12-18.

12. Make two cellophane triangles, following steps 7 and 8.

14. Put the paper shapes (or sequins and beads) into the envelope.

15. Seal the open side of the envelope with clear sticky tape.

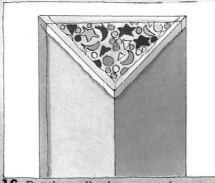

16. Put the cellophane envelope over the open end of the tube and fix it in place with clear sticky tape.

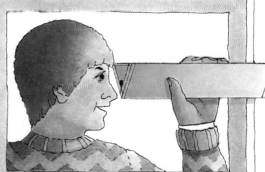

17. Look toward the light through the paper-covered end of the tube.

18. Shake the tube and look again to see a different pattern.

Colour

Sunlight looks 'white', but it is really made up of different colours. These colours are red, orange, yellow, green, blue, indigo (blue-purple) and violet. Together, they form a band called the spectrum. We see an object in a certain colour because that colour is reflected by the object, while other colours are absorbed. Colour experiments are endlessly fascinating, as you will find when you dip into this chapter.

Whizzer wheel

Spinning this coloured disc takes some practice. But once you master the art, you'll have an interesting toy that also proves an important scientific fact about light.

Materials

- stiff, white card 25cm square
- scissors, ruler and pencil
- pair of compasses and protractor
- paint brush and poster paints in red, orange, yellow, green, blue and violet
- 1m fine string

1. Draw a circle with a radius of 10cm (see p.7) on the card.

2. Cut out this circle

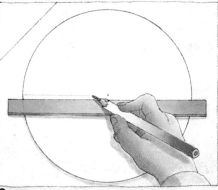

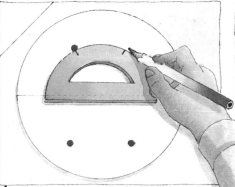

3. Draw a line through the centre of the circle to divide it in half.

4. Measure and mark 60° angles in each half of the circle (see p.7).

5. Draw diagonal lines through these marks to divide the circle into six equal segments.

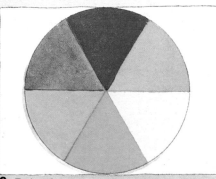

6. Paint the segments of the circle in this order: red, orange, yellow, green, blue and violet. Let the paint dry.

7. With the tip of the scissors, make two holes, about 1.5cm apart, on either side of the centre.

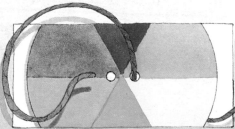

8. Thread the string up through one hole and down through the other.

9. Tie the ends and trim the knot.

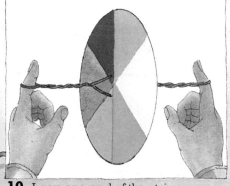

10. Loop one end of the string over each index finger and flip the disc until the string is tightly twisted.

11. Steadily pull apart your hands to make the disc spin rapidly. Move your hands inward as the disc slows down, then pull them apart again. Practise these movements until you can keep the disc spinning.

When the disc spins quickly, you will see only a creamy colour. That's because your eye cannot pick out separate colours at speed.

The disc also shows that 'white' light consists of several colours. In fact, all light is made up of red, orange, yellow, green, blue, indigo and violet. (If you divided the disc into seven segments and painted the seventh segment indigo, you would see pure white light.)

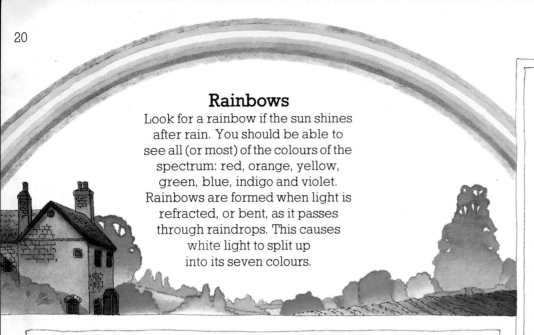

Rainbows

Look for a rainbow if the sun shines after rain. You should be able to see all (or most) of the colours of the spectrum: red, orange, yellow, green, blue, indigo and violet. Rainbows are formed when light is refracted, or bent, as it passes through raindrops. This causes white light to split up into its seven colours.

Colour pyramid

Everyone knows that when colours are mixed, new colours are made. But try this experiment to see what effect coloured screens, or filters, have on particular colours. You will find that the colour pyramid is also a very beautiful model to keep.

Feathery fringes

You can split up 'white' light by diffraction, to see the individual colours of the spectrum. Diffraction is caused by light passing through narrow openings. Do this experiment in a darkened room.

Materials
● candle in candle-holder
● matches
● bird's feather

1. Put the candle-holder on a safe and solid surface.

 2. Ask an adult to light the candle and darken the room.

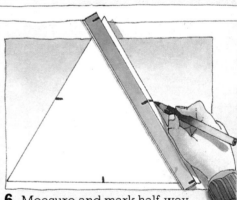

6. Measure and mark half-way along each side of the triangle.

3. Stand about 30cm away from the candle and shut one eye.

4. Hold the feather in front of your other eye and look through it at the candle flame.

You will see several images, each with a fringe of rainbow colours. The candlelight splits up into these colours as it passes through the narrow slits in the feather.

5. Still holding the feather, slowly move back from the candle to see even more images of the flame.

6. Rotate the feather to make the images of the flame revolve, too. (Blow out the candle flame.)

10. Lay one of the cut-out triangles on one of the sheets of cellophane.

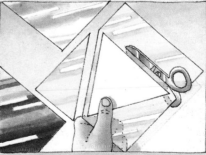

11. Cut a cellophane triangle 1cm larger than the triangular pattern.

12. Repeat steps 10 and 11 using the other sheets of cellophane.

Materials

- stiff, white card 35cm square
- pencil, ruler and protractor
- scissors
- modelling knife
- sheets of red, yellow, colourless and blue cellophane, each 12cm square
- clear glue
- clear sticky tape

1. Draw a straight line 30cm long at the bottom of the card.

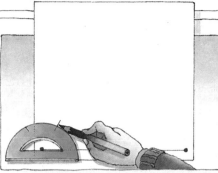

2. Put the centre of the protractor on one end of the line and mark the 60° angle, as shown.

3. Repeat step 2 on the other end of the line.

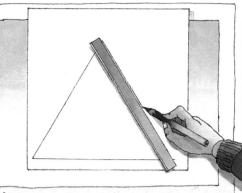

4. Draw straight lines from the ends of the line through the points marked.

5. Cut out the triangle.

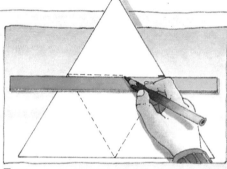

7. Draw dotted lines to join up the marks you have made. This makes four smaller triangles.

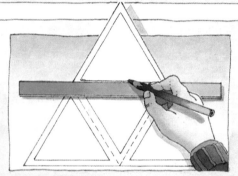

8. Measure and draw borders 1cm wide inside each of these four smaller triangles.

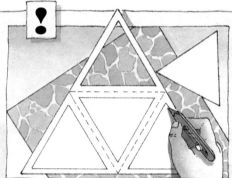

9. Use the modelling knife to cut out the solid-line triangles, as shown. This makes four small windows.

13. Neatly glue a cellophane triangle over each window.

14. Write the name of the colour below each cellophane window.

15. Guided by the ruler, pull the tip of the scissors along the dotted lines to score them.

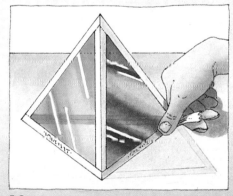

16. Fold the card on the dotted lines and tape the pyramid edges together with clear sticky tape.

This shape is called a tetrahedron.

17. Look through one window toward the light. Twist and turn the model to see different colours.

The windows filter light, allowing only certain colours through. Blue lets blue, magenta (dark pink) and green pass. Red allows only red, magenta and orange. Yellow allows yellow, orange and green. Red and yellow filters combined allow only orange, the colour common to both, to pass. Which colour combinations enable you to see green and magenta?

Light mix

Mixing coloured light doesn't give the same results as mixing paints. Ask a friend to help you hold the torches, and experiment together.

Materials
- 3 strong torches or lamps
- pieces of red, blue and green cellophane, each big enough to cover the bulb end of a torch
- sticky tape
- white card 30cm square
- white toy or ornament

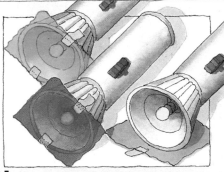

1. Tape one piece of cellophane over the bulb end of each torch.

2. Switch on the torches. Make sure the room is dark.

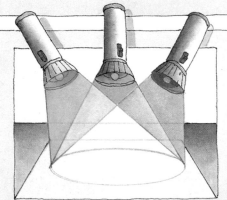 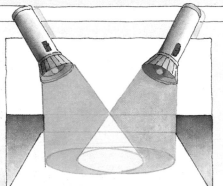

3. Shine the three torches on to the card so that the red, green and blue light beams meet.

Where the beams meet, they make white light. Red, blue and green are called the primary colours of light. That means you can make any colour from combinations of these three.

4. Now shine the red and green torches on to the card.

Where the beams meet, you will see yellow. Yellow is a secondary colour of light, or one made by mixing two primary colours. There are two other secondary colours: magenta (dark pink) and cyan (green-blue).

5. Try mixing blue and green light, then blue and red light, to discover which combination makes magenta and which makes cyan.

6. Put the white toy in the centre of the card and shine the three coloured torches on it.

7. Keeping the three light beams together, walk round the toy to see it in different colours.

3-D glasses

You can have a lot of fun with these glasses. The coloured eye-pieces act as filters, stopping certain colours from reaching your eyes.

Materials
- tracing paper 7cm × 22cm
- soft (2B) and hard (3H) pencils
- stiff, white card 7cm × 44cm
- scissors and modelling knife
- clear sticky tape
- pieces of red and green cellophane, each 6cm square
- 2 sheets white paper
- red and green pencils

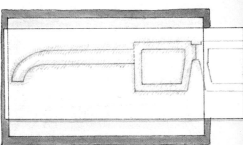

6. Reverse the tracing paper and lay it on the card so that the tracing and the outline on the card join up.

7. Repeat step 5.

8. Cut out the cardboard shape.

14. Put on the glasses.

15. Shut one eye and look at the red drawing through the red cellophane eye-piece.

The drawing will disappear! White light travels from the paper to your eye. But the red cellophane stops all colours except the red in white light. This makes the white paper look red, and so it is impossible to distinguish from the red drawing.

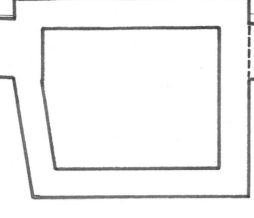

1. Lay the tracing paper over the trace pattern on this page.

2. Trace the outline of the pattern with the hard pencil. Don't forget to trace the dotted line.
Lift off the tracing paper.

3. Turn the paper over and shade across all the traced lines with the soft pencil.

4. Lay the tracing paper, shaded side down, on the white card.

5. With the hard pencil, draw over the lines on the tracing paper.

When you lift off the tracing paper, you will see the glasses shape outlined on the card.

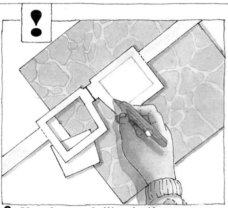

9. Use the modelling knife to cut out each eye-piece.

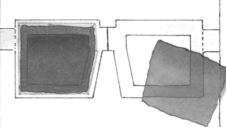

10. Stick red cellophane over one eye-piece and green over the other.

11. Guided by the ruler, pull the tip of the scissors along the dotted lines to score them.
Fold up along the dotted lines.

12. Using the red pencil, draw a picture on one sheet of paper.

13. Draw another picture with the green pencil on the other sheet of paper.

16. Shut one eye and look at the red drawing through the green cellophane eye-piece.

The green filter allows only green light to reach your eye, but as there is no green in your red drawing, it will look black.

17. Try looking at the green drawing through the green eye-piece.

18. Then look at the green drawing through the red filter.

19. Now look at some red and green pictures or objects in your room, to make them disappear or change colour.

20. If you watch a colour film through these glasses, you'll get an amazing 3-D effect!

Artificial light

Without some form of artificial light, you would have to go to bed when the sun went down! In ancient times, people used fires, oil lamps and candles made from animal fats or beeswax to provide artificial light. Today, we use mainly electricity. In this chapter, batteries provide the power for the experiments that show you how to 'create' your own light.

Signalling light

You can use this battery-run toy to flash signals to a friend or to light up a dolls' house or model.

Materials

- about 50cm standard 2-core plastic-covered flex
- penknife and scissors
- length of strip connector
- small screwdriver
- small on-off switch
- 2 small 1.5 volt transistor radio batteries in holder
- 2.5 volt light bulb in holder

1. Loosen the screws in the bulb holder.

2. Unscrew the cover on the switch and loosen the screws inside.

3. Use scissors to cut between the two cores of flex at both ends, then pull apart the cores until about 3cm are separated at both ends.

4. Use scissors to strip off 1cm of plastic from the four 3cm-lengths. You will find lots of fine strands of shiny wire underneath.

5. Twist these fine strands into four single strands.

6. Wind each single strand on one end of the flex round each of the screws in the bulb holder. Tighten the two screws.

7. Wind one of the single strands on the other end of the flex round one screw in the switch. Tighten this screw.

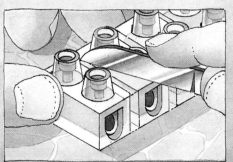

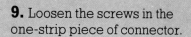

8. Use the penknife to cut one strip from the length of connector.

9. Loosen the screws in the one-strip piece of connector.

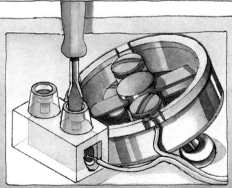

10. Push the spare single strand under one screw in the connector. Tighten this screw.

11. Strip off 1cm of plastic from both the black wire (the negative) and the red wire (the positive) attached to the battery. Twist the strands of shiny wire together.

12. Wind the single strand on the black wire round the spare screw in the switch. Tighten this screw.

13. Screw the cover back on to the switch.

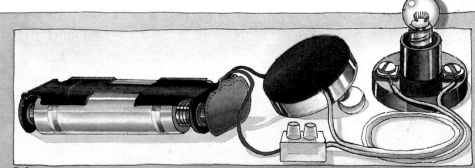

14. Push the single strand on the red wire under the spare screw in the connector. Tighten this screw.

Simply turn the switch on and off to flash signals. You could even signal in Morse code, if you used a library book for reference.

Flashing badge

A battery-run badge which flashes on and off is a unique toy. It is not difficult to make, although there are a lot of steps, and the end result is absolutely dazzling!

Materials

- about 1m standard 2-core plastic-covered flex
- penknife and scissors
- 3 volt light-emitting diode
- 270 ohm resistor
- small doorbell switch
- 2 small 1.5 volt transistor radio batteries in holder
- length of strip connector
- small screwdriver
- sewing needle threaded with 70-80cm strong cotton thread
- large safety pin
- photograph or magazine picture of a face, about 6cm square
- stiff card 6cm square and glue
- double-sided sticky tape.

1. Follow steps 3-5 of 'Signalling light' (see p.25).

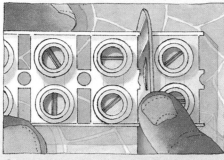

2. Use the penknife to cut the strip connector into a three-strip length and a one-strip length.
Put the one-strip length aside.

3. Loosen all the screws in the three-strip connector.

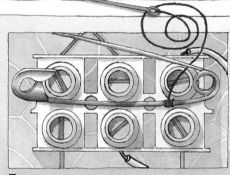

7. Tie the spare end of the thread to the fixed bar of the safety pin, then lay the open pin along the middle of the connector.

8. Sew the safety pin into place by passing the needle down through one hole, across the bottom of the connector, up through the second hole and round the other end of the pin. Then sew this 'u'-shaped route in reverse. Repeat until the pin is firmly fixed to the connector.
Trim the knot and close the pin.

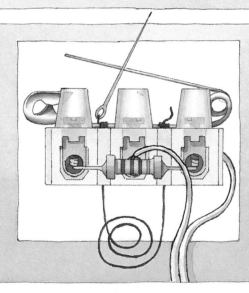

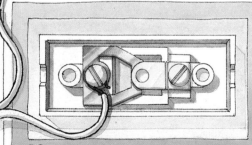

13. Wind one single strand on the unconnected end of the flex round one screw in the switch.
Tighten this screw.

14. Follow step 11 of 'Signalling light' (see p.25) to strip the wires fixed to the battery.

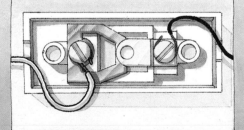

15. Wind the single strand on the black battery wire (the negative) round the spare screw in the switch.
Tighten this screw.

16. Loosen the screws on the one-strip connector.

17. Push the single strand on the red battery wire (the positive) under the screw in the one-strip connector, as shown.
Tighten this screw.

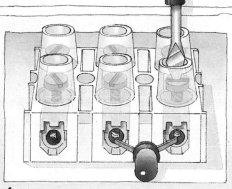

4. Bend the diode's terminals (the wire extensions) and push them under the two connector screws shown.
Tighten these two screws.

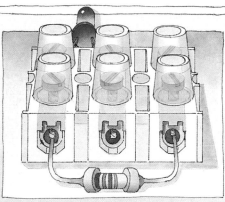

5. Bend the two terminals of the resistor and push them under the two connector screws shown.
Tighten these two screws.

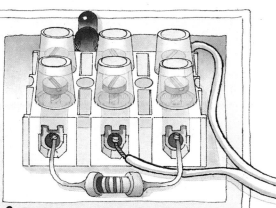

6. Push each single strand on one end of the flex into the remaining two positions in the connector.
Tighten these two screws.

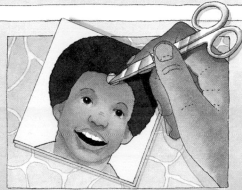

9. Glue the photograph to the card, let the glue dry, and then punch a small hole in the forehead.

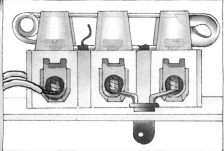

10. Push the diode's head through the hole from the back of the card. (Bend the terminals, if necessary.)

11. Press a strip of double-sided sticky tape to the bottom of the connector. Peel off the backing paper, then press the other sticky side to the back of the card.
Do this very carefully, so that you do not damage the diode when you lift up the connector.

12. Loosen the screws in the switch.

18. Push the single strand of the spare core of flex under the other connector screw.
Tighten this screw.

19. Press the button. If the light does not come on, reverse the black and red battery wire connections.

Pin the card to your clothes and run the flex under them so that the switch and battery are in a pocket. Press and release the button on the switch to make your badge flash.

Tricks of light

Light can play some astonishing tricks. A rainbow, for instance, is a trick of colour. A straight stick looks bent in water, because light is refracted (or bent) when it passes from air to water or water to air. In fact, light is always refracted when it passes from one material to another of different density, or 'heaviness'. Your own eyes can deceive you, too! The experiments in this chapter show several tricks played by both light and sight.

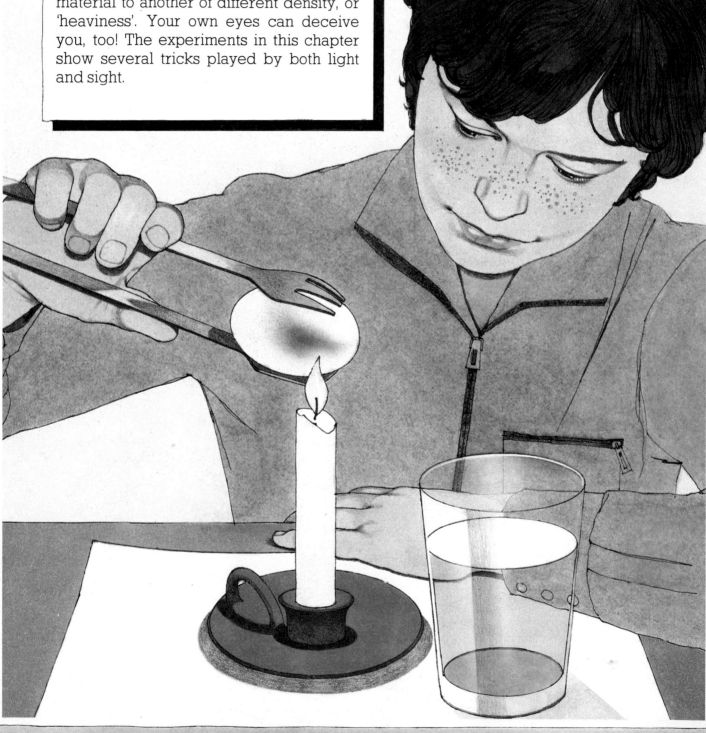

Silvery egg

In this experiment, you can make a black egg look silvery. It sounds impossible, but it's true!

Materials
- unshelled, hard-boiled egg
- candle in candle-holder
- matches
- pair of tongs
- glass of water

1. Light the candle.

2. Grasp the egg firmly with the tongs.

3. Hold the egg in the candle flame, turning it until it is completely covered with soot. Blow out the candle flame.

4. Gently lower the egg into the glass of water.

The centre of the egg will look black because light travels in a straight line to the soot. But tiny pockets of air have been trapped between the soot and the water. Light travelling from the water to these air pockets is refracted (or bent) away from the soot, and so you see only a silvery halo.

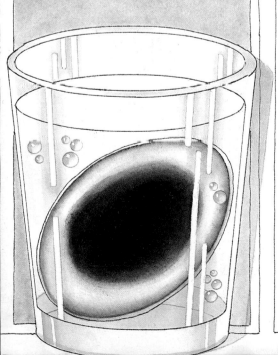

Optical illusions

Magicians often rely upon illusions, or tricks of sight, to fool their audiences. Here are some magical tricks for you to do, based on the fact that light travels at different speeds through different materials.

Materials
- glass with straight sides
- jug of water
- teaspoon
- cup and coin

1. Half-fill the glass with water and put the teaspoon into it.

2. Hold the glass so that it is level with your eyes.

The spoon seems to be broken at the boundary between air and water because light is refracted, or bent, as it passes from air to water. Water also magnifies the spoon.

3. Put the cup on a flat surface and put the coin into it.

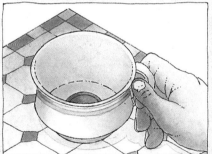

4. Slowly move the cup away from you until the coin suddenly passes beyond your line of vision.

5. Keep quite still and ask someone to pour water into the cup until you can see the coin again.

When the level of the water is raised, light travelling from the coin can be refracted at a higher point, and so reach your eye. The coin also seems to be higher in the cup. That's because light travels more slowly in water than in air.

Shrunken legs

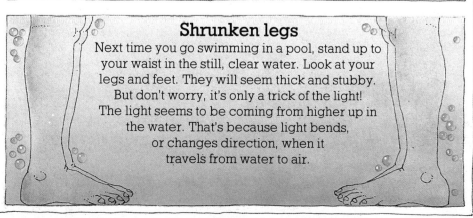

Next time you go swimming in a pool, stand up to your waist in the still, clear water. Look at your legs and feet. They will seem thick and stubby. But don't worry, it's only a trick of the light! The light seems to be coming from higher up in the water. That's because light bends, or changes direction, when it travels from water to air.

Mini movies

Your eye cannot pick out different colours if they are moving rapidly. The 'Whizzer wheel' (see pp. 18-19) proves this. The same is true of moving pictures. Here's a way to see how a cinematic film works.

Materials
- tracing paper 7cm × 10cm
- soft (2B) and hard (3H) pencils
- white writing paper 4cm × 18cm

1. Lay the tracing paper over the drawings and trace them with the hard pencil. Lift off the paper.

2. Turn the paper over and shade across all the traced lines with the soft pencil.

3. Fold the writing paper in half.

4. Lay the tracing of the upper drawing, shaded side down, in the middle of the first 'page'.

5. Using the hard pencil, draw over the traced lines.

6. Lay the tracing of the lower drawing, shaded side down, in the middle of the second 'page'.

7. Repeat step 5, then pencil over the outlines.

8. Holding the folded edge in one hand, roll the first 'page' tightly round the pencil. Rapidly move the pencil back and forth across the 'page' to see a moving picture.

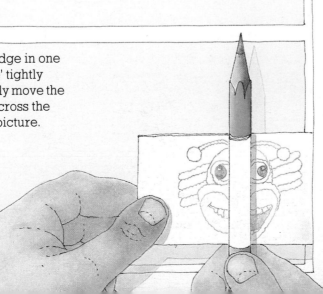

Stroboscope

Normally, you cannot see the spokes of a moving bicycle wheel or the blades of a rapidly turning fan. But a stroboscope enables you to see such things in slow motion!

Materials
- stiff, white card 26cm square, painted black on one side
- pair of compasses
- ruler and coloured pencils

8. Put the ruler across a straight line at the 6cm-radius circle.

9. Measure and mark 0.5cm on either side of the straight line.

15. Glue the cotton reel to the centre of the card. Let the glue dry.

16. Rub about 3cm of one end of the dowelling with soap.

- protractor
- scissors and modelling knife
- empty cotton reel
- 20cm dowelling, or long pencil, to fit into cotton reel
- strong, clear glue
- bar of soap
- smaller washer and drawing pin

1. Draw a circle with a radius of 12cm (see p.7) on the white side of the card.

2. Draw a second circle with a radius of 11cm.

3. Draw a third circle with a radius of 6cm.

4. Cut out the disc, following the outermost circle.

5. Draw a line through the centre of the disc to divide it in half.

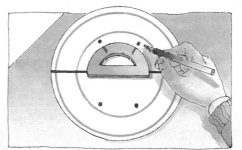

6. Measure and mark 60° angles in each half of the circle (see p.7).

7. Draw diagonal lines through the marks to divide the circle into six.

10. Move the ruler to the 11cm-radius circle and repeat step 9.

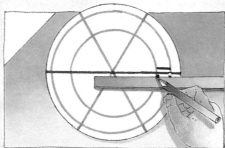

11. With the ruler parallel to the straight line, draw lines to join the points you have marked.

12. Repeat steps 8-11 on the other straight lines.

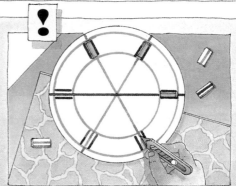

13. Use the modelling knife to cut out these 1cm-wide slats.

14. Turn the card over so that the black side faces up.

17. Push the soaped end into the cotton reel.

18. Put the washer under the head of the drawing pin.

19. Push the pin through the card so that it goes into the dowelling.

20. Hold the dowelling in one hand so that the black side of the disc is about 25cm in front of your eyes.

21. Spin the disc and look through it at a moving object or person.

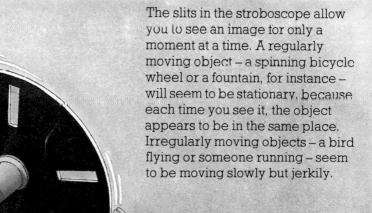

The slits in the stroboscope allow you to see an image for only a moment at a time. A regularly moving object – a spinning bicycle wheel or a fountain, for instance – will seem to be stationary, because each time you see it, the object appears to be in the same place. Irregularly moving objects – a bird flying or someone running – seem to be moving slowly but jerkily.

32

False images

This experiment shows you the kind of optical tricks you might like to try first, and then show to your friends. You'll get some laughs.

Materials
- pencil
- sheet of writing paper
- ruler and sticky tape

1. Lightly hold the blunt end of the pencil between your thumb and index finger.

2. Waggle your hand so the pencil tip moves quickly up and down.

You'll see a very rubbery pencil!

3. Roll the paper into a tube with a diameter of about 5cm (see p.7), and fix it with sticky tape.

4. With your eyes open, put one end of the tube over your right eye.

5. Hold your left hand upright half-way along the tube and look at it with your left eye.

You'll notice that something is missing!

6. Hold your two index fingers about 1cm apart and about 30cm in front of your eyes. Focus your eyes on a distant object, such as a wall.

You will see another image floating between your fingers.

7. Move your fingers slightly together, then apart, to get different effects.

Brain teasers

Most optical illusions are the result of not seeing an object or situation accurately. Sometimes we see only the things that we are used to seeing, ignoring images or positions of images that seem strange to us. The eyes send information, via the optic nerve, to the brain. Sometimes the brain translates the information wrongly. See what your eyes and brain make of these images!

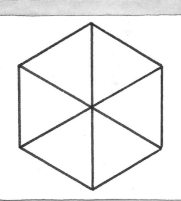

2. Is it possible to decide whether this figure is a cube or a flat hexagon (six-sided figure)?

The answer is no!

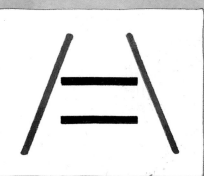

3. Are the central black lines of equal length or not?
Measure the lines to see if you have guessed correctly.

1. Look at the two drawing on the right and try to decide whether they are the same length or not. Measure them with a ruler to see if you were right.

We see the upper drawing as being nearer to the eye than the lower one, so the pictures are distorted. This means that the brain misinterprets the information it receives from our eyes.

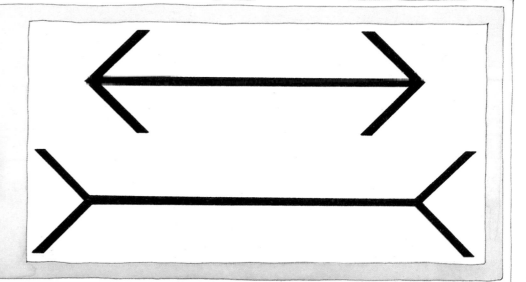

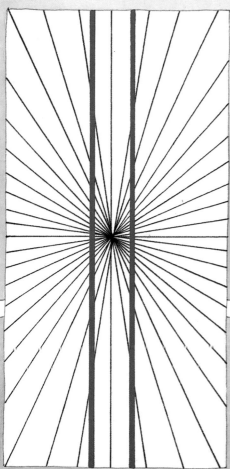

4. These two red lines seem to bend and bulge because the black lines fanning out behind distort them. In fact, the red lines are parallel. Check with a ruler!

5. Cut out a piece of card about 4cm wide and 13cm long. Hold the card upright along the dotted line between these two pictures. Lower your face to the edge of the card so that each eye can see an image on either side of the card. Did you see something move?

When you look at an object, each eye sees a different part of it. The brain mixes the two images so that you have the impression of seeing one image. Although each eye sees one of the pictures above, your brain is busy doing its work of mixing the images together.

Light and shadow

Day and night or light and shadow make our world interesting. Shadow is really an absence of light, formed when light is stopped by an opaque object – that is, one you cannot see through. Photography and printing make fascinating use of light and shadow. Many of the experiments in this chapter show how these processes work, and you can keep the results of several experiments for a long time.

Shadow portraits

Portraits in shadow are known as silhouettes. Ask two or more friends to help you make some. You can frame the portraits or arrange them on a pinboard.

Materials
- chair and torch
- 3 sheets white paper, each 40cm square
- masking tape and scissors
- pencil and ruler

4. Switch on the torch, then close the door, pull down blinds or draw curtains to darken the room.

5. Shine the torch on the seated friend so that his or her head is outlined in shadow on the paper.

12. Put double-sided sticky tape on one side of the card.

13. Peel off the backing paper.

- black poster paint
- paint brush
- modelling knife
- 3 sheets stiff, coloured card, each 40cm square
- double-sided sticky tape
- ribbon or string

1. Put the chair very close to one wall of a room.

2. Seat one of your friends on the chair, facing sideways.

3. Use masking tape to fix one sheet of paper to the wall behind the person's head.

6. Ask another friend to outline the shadow with pencil.

7. Take down the paper.

8. Repeat steps 1-7 to outline your other friend and yourself.

9. Lighten the room and carefully paint inside the outline on each sheet of paper.
Let the paint dry.

10. Draw lines 2.5cm in from each edge of one sheet of card.

11. With the modelling knife and ruler, cut along these lines.

14. Press the card, sticky side down, on one of the sheets of white paper so that the painted profile is in the centre of it.

15. With the tip of the modelling knife, make a hole in each of two corners of the card.

16. Thread the ribbon through the holes and knot the ends at the back. The portrait is ready to hang up.

17. Repeat steps 10-16 to frame the other two portraits.

Shadow game

You can have some fun identifying shadows at home.

Materials
- chair and torch
- everyday objects such as keys, scissors, a cup, fork or whisk

1. Ask someone to sit on a chair facing a wall.

2. Switch on the torch and darken the room.

3. Stand behind the seated person and shine the torch on the wall.

4. Hold one object in front of the torch so that a shadow falls on the wall. With practise, you can hold and turn the object so that its shadow is difficult to recognise.

The winner is the first person to recognise the shadow!

You and your shadow

Watch your shadow the next time you walk along an illuminated street at night. If the source of light is close, your shadow will be short. If you move away from the light, your shadow will lengthen. Your shadow will 'copy' your actions. See what happens when you try to jump on it!

Pinhole camera

The earliest camera was rather like the one you make in this experiment. It was simply a box with a tiny hole in one side. Light passed through the hole and cast an upside-down image inside the box. But the image could not be fixed. There's an extra thrill in making a pinhole camera, because you can record the image on modern photographic paper. When you have made the camera, follow 'Pinhole photographs' (see pp.42-43) to make prints.

Materials
- cardboard box with lid, at least 10cm high between lid and base
- pencil and ruler
- pair of compasses
- scissors and modelling knife
- black poster paint
- paint brush
- thick, black paper 4cm square
- masking tape
- straight pin
- tracing paper 2cm larger than base of box
- dark cloth at least 60cm square
- 2 or 3 safety pins

1. Put the lid of the box aside.

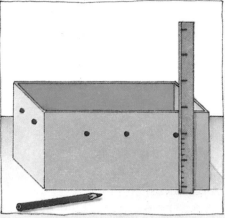

2. Use the pencil and ruler to mark points 10cm from the base on every side of the box.

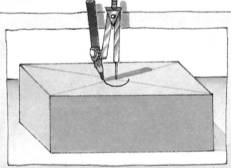

8. Put the point of the compasses on the centre, and draw a circle with a radius of 1.5cm (see p.7).

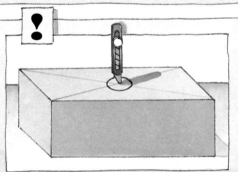

9. Using the tip of the modelling knife, carefully cut out this circle to make a round hole.

10. Paint the inside of the box and lid black.
Let the paint dry, then put the lid aside until your are ready to take photographs (see pp.42-43).

14. Hold the box at eye level so that you are looking into the screen.

15. Ask a friend to pin the cloth round your head and the camera, so that only the pinhole is visible.

16. Point the pinhole out of the window at a scene. Move back and forth until you see a clear image of the view on the screen.

If you have blocked all light from your eyes and the screen, you should see a clear upside-down image. Light from the top of the view passes in a straight line

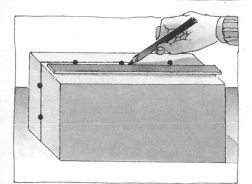

3. Using the ruler to guide you, draw straight lines between these points, all the way round the box.

4. With the scissors, cut from the top of the box to the 10cm line.

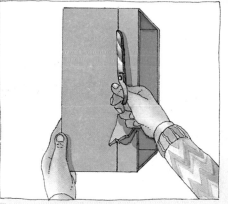

5. Then cut along the 10cm line all the way round the box.

6. Turn the box bottom side up.

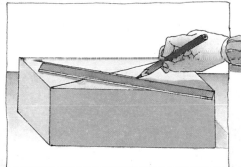

7. Draw two straight lines to join the opposite corners of the box.

These lines are called diagonals, and the point where they cross is the centre of the bottom of the box.

11. Tape the black paper over the hole, on the inside of the box. Use tape along all sides of the paper so that it is sealed completely.

12. Using the point of the pin, make a tiny hole in the centre of the black paper.

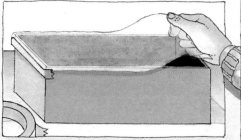

13. Tape the tracing paper over the open side of the box. This is the screen of the camera.

through the pinhole to the bottom of the screen. Light from the bottom of the view travels to the top of the screen. (A modern camera has a lens instead of a pinhole.)

Camera obscura

Imagine standing in a giant pinhole camera.
You get the same effect if you visit a *camera obscura*.
The words are Latin, and mean 'dark chamber'.
A tiny hole in one wall of the chamber
lets in light, which casts an upside-down image
of the outside view on to an inside wall or screen.
These chambers were popular before the camera
was invented, and many of them still exist.

Darkroom

Photographic printing is a totally absorbing hobby. The materials are not cheap, but your prints can be exciting and will last a long time. Photographic printing must be done in a darkroom under a red light bulb called a 'safelight'. Choose a room with small windows and running water. A bathroom is ideal. First ask if anyone needs the room, as it will take at least two hours to do a printing experiment. (See pp.40-41, 42-43 and 44-45 for printing experiments.)

Materials

- washing line and pegs
- 3 plastic trays or photographic developing trays, each about 18cm × 22cm (or slightly larger than the photographic paper you choose)
- 2 pairs plastic tongs
- sticky labels and pen
- red light bulb
- 'do not disturb' sign
- thick, black paper or polythene
- masking tape and scissors
- old blanket, tacks and hammer (optional)

1. Put the pegs on the washing line.

2. Fix the line so that it hangs over the bath. You could do this by tying the ends to towel rails, taps or any conveniently fixed objects.

3. Put the trays on the work area.

4. Clear a space near the first tray. (You can put your photographic paper and torch here when you are ready to print.)

5. Label the first tray 'developer', the second tray 'wash' and the third tray 'fixer'.

Printing chemicals

To make photographic prints (see pp.40-41, 42-43, 44-45), prepare the darkroom and take everything that you need into that room. You will not be able to open the door until you have finished. Light ruins photographic paper. Always wear surgical gloves to prepare the special chemicals that will fix the image to the paper, and be sure never to get the chemicals near your eyes or mouth.

Materials

- tight-fitting surgical gloves
- 100 ml photographic developer
- 60ml photographic fixer
- 700 ml (at least) measuring jug
- hot and cold water
- thermometer
- plastic bowl or bucket
- clock or watch with second hand

1. Put on the plastic gloves.

2. Put the thermometer into the jug.

3. Add hot and cold water to the jug until you have 600 ml of water at between 20°C and 21°C.

4. Shake the bottle of developer.

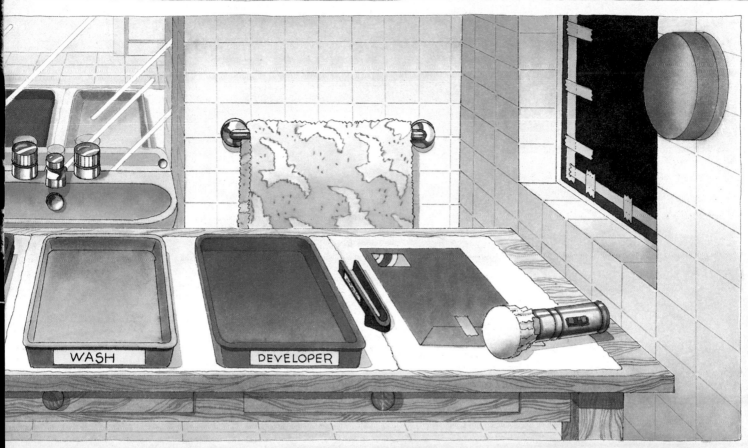

6. Label the tongs 'developer' and 'fixer'. Put them with their trays.

7. Make sure the switch is off, then put the red light bulb in the light socket. Don't take any other kind of electric light into the bathroom.

8. Switch on the red light.

9. Tape the black paper (or polythene) over the windows.

10. Hang the 'do not disturb' sign on the outside door handle, then close the door from the inside.

11. If the door lets in light, fix the blanket over the inside of it. You could do this by tacking the blanket above the door frame.

12. Now prepare your 'Printing chemicals' in the darkroom.

5. Add 100 ml of developer to the water in the jug and stir the mixture with the thermometer.

6. Pour the liquid into the tray labelled 'developer'.

7. Wash the thermometer and jug in clean, warm water.

8. Repeat steps 2 and 3.

9. Shake the bottle of fixer.

10. Add 60ml of fixer to the water in the jug and stir.

11. Pour this liquid into the tray labelled 'fixer'.

12. Repeat step 7.

13. Fill the 'wash' tray with water.

14. Put the bowl into the bath and fill it with clean, cold water.

15. Put the clock on the work area.

You are now ready to print pictures.

Contact prints

Photographic paper is specially treated with chemicals that are sensitive to light. This experiment shows the basic method of printing on photographic paper. The exposure times given here are for turning a negative piece of film into a positive print. (On a negative, everything that should be white is black; a positive shows black and white as they should be.)

Materials
- as for 'Darkroom' and 'Printing chemicals' (see pp.38-39)
- grade 3 resin-coated photographic paper
- scissors and masking tape
- torch and white writing paper
- small sheet of clean glass
- black-and-white negative
- old towel

1. Prepare the 'Darkroom' and 'Printing chemicals' (see pp.38-39).

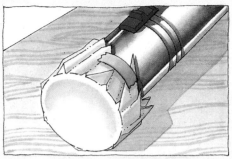

2. Tape a piece of writing paper over the bulb end of the torch. The torch should be switched off and the red light on (see pp.38-39).

7. Take off the glass and negative and put them aside.

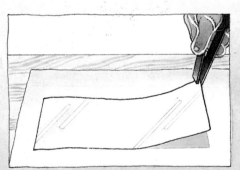

8. Pick up the photographic paper by grasping the edge of one corner with the tongs labelled 'developer'.

9. Gently lower the paper, shiny side down, into the 'developer' tray.

10. Push down the paper with the tongs to submerge it completely.

11. Using the tongs, flip the paper over so that it rests shiny side up. Put down the tongs.

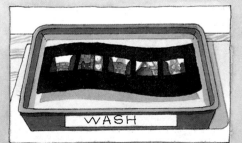

14. Submerge it in the 'wash' tray, to wash off the chemicals. Put down the tongs.

15. Gently rock the tray to and fro for about one minute.

16. Lift out the paper with the 'fixer' tongs and gently shake it.

17. Submerge the print in the tray labelled 'fixer'.

18. Put down the tongs and gently rock the tray for about one minute. Leave the print in the fixer for a few more minutes.

19. Lift out the print with the 'fixer' tongs and put it into the bowl of water in the bath. Leave it there for about 20 minutes.

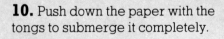

3. Make sure your hands are clean and dry, then cut a small strip from one sheet of photographic paper. This is a test piece. You need to establish exposure time before using more paper.

Keep the rest of the paper sealed in its envelope or box. This is very important. The smallest chink of light will ruin photographic paper.

4. Put this strip, shiny side up, on the work area.

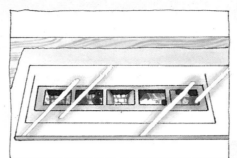

5. Lay the negative on the shiny side of the photographic paper and put the glass on top of it.

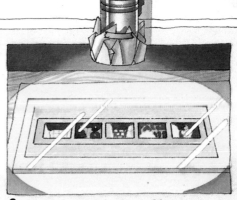

6. Hold the torch about 60cm above the paper and switch it on for 10 seconds, then switch it off. Do this once only.

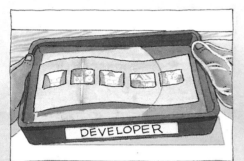

12. Gently rock the tray so that the developer moves to and fro across the paper. Do this for about one minute, or until a clear image appears on the paper and the background is very black.

The black areas are the ones you exposed to light. If your print has gone very black in the first few seconds, the paper was over-exposed. To correct this, start again at step 3, and shorten the time of exposure in step 6.

If the background does not go very black, the paper was under-exposed. To correct this, start again at step 3, and lengthen the time of exposure in step 6.

13. If your print is just right, lift it out with the 'developer' tongs and gently shake off the liquid.

20. Repeat steps 3-19 to make more prints. You can use small strips of paper or whole sheets.

21. When all the prints are in the bowl, you can open the darkroom door to let in light.

22. Run cold water into the bowl for about five minutes, swirling the prints round with your hand.

23. Gently lift out each print by one corner and peg it to the washing line. Don't let the prints touch, or you will get marks on them. Leave them to dry.

24. Pour away the chemicals and wash your equipment and the bath well.

42

Pinhole photographs

There's something very special about taking pictures with a camera you have made yourself (see pp.36-37). Use your pinhole camera on a bright day, and photograph a still scene that is mainly black-and-white, such as black railings in front of a white house.

Materials

- pinhole camera box and lid (see pp.36-37) without tracing paper screen
- as for 'Darkroom' and 'Printing chemicals' (see pp.38-39)
- grade 3 resin-coated photographic paper
- masking tape and scissors
- old towel
- torch and white writing paper
- small sheet of clean glass

1. Prepare the darkroom, making sure that only the red light is on (see pp.38-39).

2. Make sure your hands are clean and dry.

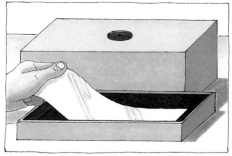

3. If necessary, trim one sheet of photographic paper so that it will fit inside the lid of the camera. Keep the rest of the paper, and any trimmings, sealed from the light.

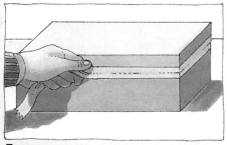

5. Tape the lid to the camera box along all the edges, to seal it completely. No light must get in.

6. Gently stick tape over the pinhole of the camera box.

7. Take the camera and clock and put them on a well-lit window sill, with the pinhole side of the camera facing a view outside.

8. Tape the camera down, as it must be kept very, very still.

11. Remove the camera and the clock, take them to the darkroom, and switch on the red light.

12. Prepare the 'Printing chemicals' (see pp.38-39).

13. Remove the lid of the camera.

14. Gently remove the tape holding the photographic paper.

15. With clean, dry hands, lift out the paper by one corner. The paper will be blank. You have to develop it to see the image.

16. To make a negative print of your picture, follow steps 8-19 and 21-23 of 'Contact prints' (see pp.40-41). On the print, everything that should be white will be black.

17. To make a positive print from the negative, repeat steps 2-24 of 'Contact prints' (see pp.40-41), using a sheet of photographic paper. Note that in step 6 you should switch on the torch for about 20 seconds.

negative print

4. Tape the paper, shiny side up, in the middle of the camera lid. Use tape along all the sides of the paper to seal out the light completely.

9. Decide on your exposure time. On a bright, sunny day allow about two minutes. On a bright, cloudy day, allow about eight minutes.

10. Peel away one corner of the masking tape to reveal the pinhole, time the exposure, and stick the tape back into position.

positive print.

Disappearing images
You can create some unusual effects by reversing the normal photographic process. Use a black-and-white photograph for this experiment.

Materials
- as for 'Darkroom' and 'Printing chemicals' (see pp.38-39)
- grade 3 resin-coated photographic paper
- scissors and masking tape
- torch and white writing paper
- small sheet of clean glass
- black-and-white photograph
- old towel

1. Prepare the 'Darkroom' and 'Printing chemicals' (see pp.38-39).

2. Follow step 2 of 'Contact prints' (see pp.40-41).

3. With clean, dry hands, trim one sheet of photographic paper to about the same size as your photograph.

4. Put this sheet, shiny side up, on the work area.
Keep the rest of the paper sealed away from the light.

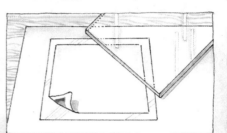

5. Lay the photograph, face down, on the photographic paper and put the sheet of glass on top of it.

6. Hold the torch about 30cm above the paper and switch it on for 15 seconds, then switch it off. Do this once only.

7. To develop a negative print, follow steps 7-19 and 21-23 of 'Contact prints' (see pp.40-41).

8. When the negative is dry, put it face down on another sheet of photographic paper.

9. Put the sheet of glass on the negative and expose the print to the torch light for 20 seconds.

10. Repeat steps 7-19 and 21-24 of 'Contact prints' (see pp.40-41).

The print will be entirely different from the original! Some details will be lost and others emphasised.

Photograms

Photograms are silhouettes printed on photographic paper. You can make them by using all kinds of objects, but small, flattish ones give the best results. Experiment with leaves, keys, paper clips, buttons, elastic bands, raw rice or seeds.

Materials

- as for 'Darkroom' and 'Printing chemicals' (see pp.38-39)
- grade 3 resin-coated photographic paper
- scissors and masking tape
- torch and white writing paper
- small, flat objects
- old towel

1. Follow steps 1-4 of 'Contact prints' (see pp.40-41).

2. Put a flat object on the strip of paper.

3. Hold the torch about 60cm above the paper and switch it on for three seconds, then switch it off. Do this once only.

4. Take the object off the paper and put it aside.

5. Follow steps 8-23 of 'Contact prints' (see pp.40-41).

You can use one flat object, or lots of objects, to print larger photograms. (Do step 24 of 'Contact prints' when you have finished.) To colour your photograms, do the 'Colour prints' experiment on the next page.

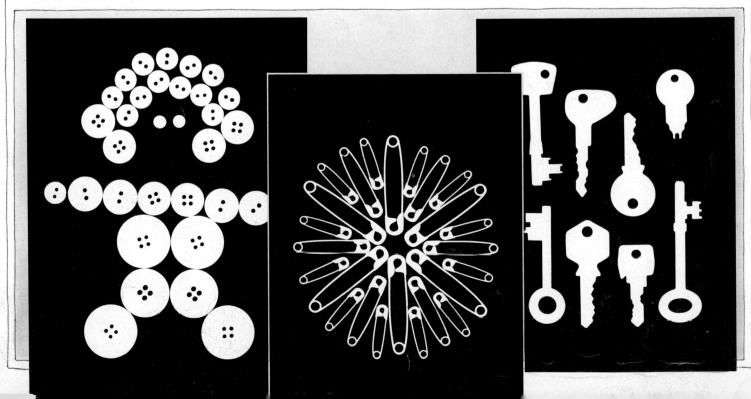

Colour prints

Colouring photograms is great fun. First, ask if you may use the bathroom for this experiment, and make sure you clean up later.

Materials
- newspaper
- black-and-white photograms
- washing line and pegs
- jug and spoon
- food dye and eye-dropper
- plastic tray or shallow bowl

1. Hang the washing line and pegs over the bath.

2. Line the bath with newspaper.

3. Put 100 ml of water in the jug.

4. Add 10-15 drops of food dye for a pale tint, or 25-30 drops for a stronger colour.

5. Stir in the colour.

6. Pour the coloured water into the tray.

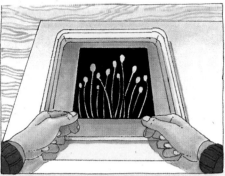

7. Slide the photogram into the tray, printed side up.

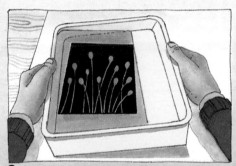

8. Gently rock the tray so that the water moves to and fro across the print. Do this for about one minute.

9. Pick up the print by one corner and shake off any excess liquid.

10. Peg the print to the washing line and leave it to drip dry.

Glossary and index

Words in CAPITAL LETTERS are also defined in the glossary.

contact print
A PHOTOGRAPHIC POSITIVE made from a PHOTOGRAPHIC NEGATIVE by putting the negative into contact with photographic paper.   see pp.40-41

cyan
A green-blue colour which is a SECONDARY colour of light, made by mixing blue and green light.   see p.22

density
The mass of a substance in relation to its volume (the amount of space it takes up).   see p.28

diffraction
The splitting up of WHITE LIGHT into the colours of the SPECTRUM, when light passes through narrow openings.   see p.20

filter
A screen which prevents a colour or colours passing through it.   see pp.20-21, 22-23

kaleidoscope
A tube in which mirrors show six symmetrical images.   see pp.16-17

magenta
A dark pink. A SECONDARY colour of light, made by mixing red and blue light.   see pp.21, 22

magnify
To increase or enlarge the apparent size of an object.   see p.28

optical illusion
A false image.   see pp.28-29, 30-31, 32-33

periscope
Tube holding mirrors. It allows you to see above a surface or round a corner.   see pp.12-13

photogram
A SILHOUETTE printed on photographic paper.   see pp.44-45

photographic negative
A piece of film on which everything that should be white is black.   see pp.40-41, 42-43

photographic positive
A print of an image which shows black and white as they should be.   see pp.40-41, 42-43

photosynthesis
The process by which energy in light is used by plants to make food.   see pp.8-9, 11

phototropism
A plant's movement towards light   see pp.10-11

pinhole camera
A box-type camera that allows light to pass through a tiny hole and cast an upside-down image inside the box.   see pp.36-37, 42-43

primary colours of light
The colours red, blue and green. Any other colour (SECONDARY colour) can be made from combinations of these three colours.   see p.22

rainbow
An arch in the sky showing the colours of the SPECTRUM, formed by REFRACTION of light passing through raindrops.   see pp.20, 28

reflection
The light one sees when light itself bounces off a surface.   see pp.12-13, 14-15, 16-17, 18

refraction
The phenomenon caused by light being bent when it passes at an angle from one medium to another of different DENSITY.   see pp.20, 28-29

secondary colours of light
Yellow, CYAN and MAGENTA, the colours obtained by mixing the PRIMARY colours of light.   see p.22

shadow
The absence of light.   see pp.34-45

silhouette
A profile, or outline, of a person or object.   see pp.34-35, 44-45

spectrum
The band of colours that make up WHITE LIGHT. The colours are red, orange, yellow, green, blue, indigo and violet.   see pp.18-19, 20

stroboscope
A device which appears to slow down or stop moving objects.   see pp.30-31

three-D (dimensional)
A flat image which seems to have depth.   see pp.22-23

white light
Natural light which looks white but is, in fact, made up of the colours of the SPECTRUM.   see pp.18-19, 20, 22-23